Lyman Haynes Low

Catalogue Of The Coins, Medals And Tokens

Lyman Haynes Low

Catalogue Of The Coins, Medals And Tokens

ISBN/EAN: 9783741126659

Manufactured in Europe, USA, Canada, Australia, Japa

Cover: Foto ©Thomas Meinert / pixelio.de

Manufactured and distributed by brebook publishing software
(www.brebook.com)

Lyman Haynes Low

Catalogue Of The Coins, Medals And Tokens

AUCTION SALE

OF

COINS AND MEDALS,

The Property of

JOHN R. GLOVER,

OF BROOKLYN, N. Y.,

AND OTHERS,

On Thursday, July 21, 1898,

AT 2 P. M.

AT THE COLLECTORS' CLUB,

351 FOURTH AVENUE, NEW YORK CITY.

CATALOGUE

OF THE

COINS, MEDALS AND TOKENS,

BELONGING TO

JOHN R. GLOVER,

OF BROOKLYN, N. Y.

TO WHICH ARE SUPPLEMENTED THE PROPERTIES OF VARIOUS PARTIES,
THE WHOLE EMBRACING

U. S. Copper and Silver Coins and Tokens, Fractional Currency, and Foreign Coins, Medals and Tokens
in Copper and Silver.

————•————

Which will be Sold by Public Auction at

The Rooms of the COLLECTORS' CLUB, 351 Fourth Ave., New York,

HENRY C. MERRY, Auctioneer,

THURSDAY, JULY 21, 1898,

AT TWO O'CLOCK.

————————

The Coins will be on Exhibition from 9.30 A. M., to 1 P. M.

————————

CATALOGUED BY

LYMAN H. LOW,

UNITED CHARITIES BUILDING, FOURTH AVENUE AND 22d STREET,
NEW YORK, N. Y.

THE SIZE OF

COINS AND MEDALS

(The closing number or that following name of coin)

In this Catalogue, is given in Millimeters.

(*Millimeters.*)

ABBREVIATIONS USED.

abt	about.	Ins.	inscription.	S.	Size.
Æ	Copper.	*l.*	left.	S. B.	Small bronze.
AR	Silver.	Lib.	Liberty.	sep.	separate. / separating.
bet.	between.	M. B.	Middle bronze.		
bril.	brilliant.	mil.	military.	std.	seated.
bzd.	bronzed.	*m. m.*	mint mark.	setd.	
Ctms.	Centimes.	mon.	monogram.	shld.	shield.
Ctvs.	Centavos.	mtd.	mounted.	sim.	similar.
C.S.	Counterstamped.	n. d.	no date.	sq.	square.
Cwn.	Crown.	O.	Obverse.	stdg.	standing.
cwnd.	crowned.	*Obv.*		supl.	supplement.
d.	Pence.	oct.	octagonal.	sup.	supported.
dbl.	double.	octag.		suptd.	
dif.	different.	pf.	proof.	Trans.	Translation.
do.	ditto.	*r.*	right.	unc.	uncirculated.
Ex.	Exergue.	R̸ / *Rev.*	Reverse.	v.	very.
ex.	extra.			var.	variety. / varieties.
G. B.	Large bronze.	*Res.*	restrike.		
gd.	good.	Rl. / Rls.	Reals.	W.m.	White metal.
hd.	head.			wrth.	wreath.

U. S. Mints are designated as follows: C., Charlotte; C. C., Carson City; D., Dahlonega; O., New Orleans; S., San Francisco; without letter, Philadelphia.

** All manner of copies, alterations and other impositions are excluded from my sales.

** There are no duplicates in any lot unless so mentioned specially.

Copies of this Catalogue giving prices realized, neatly executed in red ink, 40c.

☞ INSTRUCTIONS TO BIDDERS.

Coins and medals are sold at so much per piece, U. S. proof sets excepted. You cannot bid for one piece in a lot. If a lot contains ten pieces, and you desire to offer $2 for it, make your bid 20c. The auctioneer will accept an advance of 1 cent up to 50c., then 5c. up to $2.50, when 10c. is the limit, up to $10, and thereafter not less than 25c. Hence any bid up to 50c. can be entertained, but after that the bid must be 55c., 60c., and so on. Such offers as 53c., $1.01, and all intermediate figures are unavailable.

CATALOGUE.

———▶•◀———

1 **Colonial.** 1722 Rosa Americana ½ and 1 Penny, 1773 Virginia, 1783 Georgius Triumpho and Washington, Unity States, Mil. bust, and dbl.-headed Cents. Fair to good. 7

2 1783 Washingtons, "Unity States," togated and mil. bust, and dbl.-headed Cents. Good to about fine. 4

3 1783 Nova Constelatio, and Constellatio, 1785 as last, 1787 Fugio, "Mind your business," States United and United States. Fair to very good. 5

4 1791 Washington President. Bust *l.* ℞ Large eagle Cent. Good. 1

5 George Washington, bust *l.* "Liberty and Security Penny." n.d. Very good. 1

6 Vermont. 1787, '88 and another with Britannia rev. All "Vermon Auctori." Good. 3

7 Massachusetts. 1787 Half Cent and Cent. Indian stdg. Gd. 2

8 1788 Half Cent (a little bent), and Cent. Good. 2

9 Others, 1787, '88 Cents, fair ; and Mass. Button, late. 3

10 Connecticut. 1786 and '87 (2) Mailed busts *l.* Pronounced types. V. good. 3

11 1787 Draped busts *l.* Slight varieties. Mostly good. 8

12 New York. 1789 Mott's Token, 1794 Talbot, A. & L. Cent. V. good. 2

13 Kentucky. Cent, n.d. Pyramid of stars, к at top. Thin planchet, lettered edge. Good. 1

14   New Jersey. Cents, 1787, '88. Bust of a horse above plough.
     Maris 6D, 18M (rarity 3), 23R, 54k, 60P, 63q, 64t, 67v. Fair
     to very good.   8
15   Duplicates of the preceding. Vermont, Mass., Conn., New Jer-
     sey, Constellatios, Washington "Unity" and dbl.-hd (both
     good), etc. Poor, 3 holed.   26
16   **Half Cents.** 1794 Very good.   1
17   1,795 Thin planchet. Very fine, date strong; med. olive.   1
18   1795 Without Liberty pole. Date weak, otherwise fine. Thick
     planchet, plain edge.   1
19   1803 Light scratch, some corrosion on *rev.* Fine.   1
20   1803–56 Good, some fine.   16
21   1804–56 Unassorted duplicates of preceding. Mostly good.   20
22   **Cents.** 1793 Wreath, vine and bars. Crosby 9H. V. good,
     dent on edge.   1
23   1793 Another, same type. C. 10 I. Good, dark.   1
24   1793 Similar. Large letters in Liberty. C. 6F. V. fair.   1
25   1793 As last, also Liberty cap. Poor, but dates are plain.   2
26   1794 Hays 17. V. good, a few nicks.   1
27   1794 H. 18, 39, 49, 56. Poor and fair.   4
28   1794 H. 44. Good, rev. not quite equal to obv., rare.   1
29   1794 H. 47. Very good.   1
30   1795 Plain and lettered edge; 1796 Lib. cap. Fair to good.   3
31   1795, '96, '97, 2 each. Fair to about good.   6
32   1796 Liberty cap. Very good, nearly fine.   1
33   1797 Broad milled borders. Nearly fine; cleaned and bright-
     ened.   1
34   1797, '98 (3), 1800 (2). V. fair to good.   6
35   1798 Small, large and wide date, 1800 over 179–, and perfect
     date. Very good.   5
36   1798 (2), 1801 (5), '02 (5). Fair to good.   12
37   1801, '02, '03, '05. Good and v. good.   4
38   1803 Large $\frac{1}{100}$. Strong impression, fine.   1
39   1803 (3), '05 (2), '06, '07, '08 (2). Fair to good.   9
40   1804 Both dies broken. Good.   1
41   1804 Perfect dies, but slightly inferior to last.   1
42   1804 Very fair, date strong.   1
43   1804 Much worn, though every part of type and date distinct.   1
44   1805, '06, '07, '08, 2 each. About good.   8

45	1806, '07, '08, '10. Good.	4
46	1809 Nearly good, date strong.	1
47	1809 Poor and fair.	3
48	1810 (4), '12 (6), '14 (7). V. fair to good.	17
49	1811 over '10, not well centered. About good.	1
50	1811 Perfect date, good.	1
51	1811 Very fair to nearly good.	4
52	1811 Very fair.	4
53	1812 Large date, fine ; sm. do., but slightly inferior. 1813 Gd.	3
54	1813 Fair 1, good 2.	3
55	1814 to 1828, 2 var. of '17, 3 do. of '19, 2 do. '28. Mostly gd.	19
56	1823 About good.	1
57	1828 Large date, '30, '38, '43, '46. Good to fine.	5
58	1830 to 1843, var. '39 (3), '40, '42, '43 (2 each). Some very gd.	19
59	1839 over '36. Good, rather better than generally met with.	1
60	1849, '51, '53, '54, '55, '56 (2 var.), '57 small date. All partly bright.	8
61	1857 Small date. All partly bright.	4
62	1793 to 1814, every date excepting 1799. The '93 chain just recognizable ; wreath, v. poor ; '04, v. fair ; also 2 each of '09, '11. Poor to about good.	36
63	1816 to 1823, of the last, 5. Mostly fair to good.	41
64	1824 to 1834. Fair to good.	41
65	1835 to 1847. Good.	46
66	1848 to 1856. Good to fine.	40
67	**Silver.** Trimes. 1854 Unc. ; '55 Very good. Dimes. 1796 holed, fair ; 1814 C.S. on obv., fair.	4
68	Quarter Dols. 1804 Holed through a part of the figure 4, otherwise v. fair ; 1806 Good.	2
69	1805, '07 (2), '15, '18, '19, '20, '25. Poor to fair.	8
70	1821 Very good. 1835 Very fine.	2
71	Half Dols. 1794 Very fair.	1
72	1795 About good.	1
73	Dollars. 1795 Head, 3 leaves below eagle's wings. V. good, nearly fine.	1
74	1798 Very fair.	1
75	1799 Very good.	1
76	1836 GOBRECHT on base. Proof, faint scratches.	1
77	1836 Another, quite as last, slight edge dents.	1

78 1836 Another, considerably worn.   1
79 Proof set, 1871. 1, 2, 3, 3, 5, 5, 10, 25, 50c. and $1.00. Slight
        blemishes.   1
80 Hard Times Tokens. Jackson in safe, Merchants Ex., Turtle
        and safe, Maycock. Low 16, 22, 25, 65. Unc., all partly
        bright.   4
81 Ezra B. Sweet, 1837. Head ins. Liberty. Thick and thin
        planchet. L. 72, 73. Good, the latter nearly fine.   2
82 Others, various. Jackson walking, Boar, Jackass, Heads, Ships,
        etc. L. 4, 8, 19, 21, 24, 26, 38, 39, 40, 41, 51, 52, 53, 63, 66,
        67, 69, 70, 74, 78 (2 var.), 79, 80, 84, 88, 89, 90, 93. Good
        to fine.   28
83 Duplicates of the preceding, about 14 varieties. Good.   31
84 Store Cards, dated, 1833, '34, '35, '36, '37. Includes Benedict
        & Burnham, Hathaway, Smith's Clock Est., Walsh, etc. Mostly
        very good.   16
85 Others, political, of same period. Civilian bust of Jackson, an-
        other draped and laur. Verplanck bust *l.* In my new edi-
        tion H. T. T., Nos. 3, 4, 16. Fine. Brass.   3
86 Mil. bust of Jackson within wreath. AND. JACKSON PRESIDENT
        OF THE UNITED STATES 1833. ℞ Eagle within wreath. New
        ed., No. 5. Unc. Uncommon in any condition; very rare
        when so choice.   1
87 Store Cards of 1837 period, undated (including N. Y. & H.
        R. R., octagonal), with later ones 1846–60. Good to fine.   30
88 Spering, Good & Co., 138 Market st., Phila. Good. Brass.   1
89 Hart & Co. (Æ and W.m.); Lyons, New Orleans. Brass and
        plated (2 obv. dies). Leighton, N. O. and N. Y., 4 metals.
        All unc.   9
90 Duplicates of Store cards, etc. (11). Dbl-headed Cents for
        cheating (3). The poor and pierced (12).   26
91 Small Cents, 1857 (3), '58, eagle and Indian head (the latter a
        pattern), '59, Two Cents 1864, different obv. dies. V. fine to
        unc.   8
92 Encased Postage Stamps, Drake's Plantation Bitters, 10c., No.
        Am. Life Ins., 1c. Fine.   2
93 War Tokens. New York City and State; merchants' names, and
        some with devices only. A few in brass, 1 in rubber. Mostly
        unc.   78

94 Culled from the last lot ; 9 are in duplicate. Mostly unc.   35
95 Medals. Genl. George Washington. ℞ Born, etc., in 4 lines.
    Also Filmore, Fremont, Buchanan (last 3 holed) and McClel-
    lan. Good to fine. All W.m. 34 to 44.   5
96 Lafayette. Bust *l*., in gilt, on obv. and rev., without legend.
    Die proj. loop and ring. V. fine. Æ 14.   1
97 Franklin, Jackson, Verplanck, Harrison, Clay, Pierce, Kos-
    suth, etc. Mostly fine, 7 holed, probably as issued. 23 to
    41.   13
98 Filmore, Fremont, Buchanan, all bust *r*. and in brass, usually
    holed (these are not), McClellan, bust facing, rev. eagle. Æ,
    B. and W.m. Perfect.   6
99 New York Crystal Palace, 1853, by *Dowler* of Birm., 51 ;
    Atlantic Telegraph, 1858, both W.m. Also Calendars in
    brass, 1853, by Hyde ; 1854, by Pierson, both New York.
    All fine.   4
100 Miscellaneous. Chas. II, 1679, 3d. ; Anne, 1709, 2d. ; Li-
    beria Cent, 1833, etc., including some choice spiel marks, 2
    holed.   22

---

101 Half Cents. 1794, '95 (plain and lettered edge), '97 (2 var.)
    Poor and fair.   5
102 1800, '03, '04, '05, '06, '07, '08. Fair to good.   7
103 1810, '11 (both poor), '25, '26, '28 (2 var.), '29, '32, '33, '34,
    '35. Good to very fine, some in light olive.   12
104 1849, '50, '51, '53, '54, '55, '56, '57. Fine to about unc.   8
105 Duplicates of Half Cents, 20 different dates. Mostly very
    good, 1 holed.   28
106 Cents. 1794 Hays 7. Very good.   1
107 1796 Fillet head. Broad milled borders. V. good.   1
108 1797 (2 var.), '98 over '97, 1813. V. fair to good.   4
109 1816, '22, '26, '27 (2), '35, '37, '38 (2) '39, '40, '42, '45 to '52,
    '54, '55, '57, small and large date. Good to fine.   27
110 1838 Uncirculated, light olive.   1
111 Trimes. 1851 to '61, excepting '55. Good to fine.   11
112 Dimes. 1805, '07 (both holed), '07, '14 (good), '20 (2). Poor
    and fair.   6
113 1830, '31, '32, '34 (2, one very choice), '35, '37 (3 var.). Fair
    to very good.   9

114 1839, '40, '41, '42, '43, '45, '50 (2), '53 (2 var.).   Fair to about
     fine.   10
115 1846 Very fair, scarce.   1
116 1854, '56 (O. and P. mints), '57 (2), '58, '60, '61, '62 (2), '63,
     '65, '67, '71, '73, '75.   Mostly good to fine, some unc.   16
117 1876 C. C., '79, '80, '81, '83 to '87, '89, '90, '91, '93.   4 dupli-
     cates, unc. and proof.   18
118 Twenty Cents. 1875 S. mint, 1876, fine.   Quarter Dol. 1879
     Proof, slightly impaired.   3

---

119 **Copper Coins.** Half Cents, 1804, '05.   Cents, 1802, '03,
     '10, '12 and various other dates to 1845, some in duplicate.
     Mostly poor and fair, few good to fine.   76
120 Others, 1846–57, both inclusive.   Fair, some good.   122
121 Foreign Copper Coins.   Includes Antwerp, 1814 Siege, Stras-
     burg, 1814, Henneberg, etc., 16th to 19th century.   Fair to
     fine.   80
122 The poor and holed, 12 of the latter, one-half are U. S. Cents,
     a few Colonials, others miscellaneous Foreign, including 18
     small and very poor Roman coins said to have been "found
     in refuse heaps in an ancient lead mine in Germany formerly
     worked by the Romans."   110
123 **Base Coins.** A very gen'l asst., including Hy IV of Spain,
     with bust; Edinburg, Mary I, Jas. VI; Sweden, John 3d,
     and many others of interest.   The German prevail.   Some
     are poor, though mostly good to fine.   140
124 **Silver Coins.** Quar. Dol., 1831.   Good.   Half Dol., 1795.
     Poor. 1840, O. mint. V. good.   3
125 ST. CHARLES — J. J. F. ℞ LOUISVILLE — KY. V. fair, rare. 13½.   1
126 Mexico. 1871 Balance Peso. Fine. U. S. of New Grenada.
     1861 Bogota Peso. Good.   2
127 Peru. 1884 Sol. Chili. 1876 Peso. Fine.   2
128 Norway. 1849 ½ Species. Fine. Prussia. 1814 Reichs Thlr. Gd.   2
129 Spain. Amadeus, 1871 5 Pesetas. About fine.   1
130 Germany, Bohemia, Poland, etc., including 3 of Cologne by
     Heinrich, Bishop Pilgrim 1024, with Bracteates of Mayence
     and other cities.   Mostly early.   Size of 5 to 50c.   Good,
     some fine, several are base.   26

131 Bavaria. Lud. II, 1871 Gulden. Fine. Coburg-Gotha. Ernst,
1830 ⅔ Thlr. Good.   2
132 Frankfort, 1861. Nassau. Wm., 1839. Guldens. Both v. fine.   2
133 Saxony. Anton, 1827 ⅔ Thlr. Fine. Wurtemburg. Gulden.
Good.   2
134 Switzerland. ½, 1 Franc, 1881, '51. Ragusa, 1685. Venice,
And. Contarini. 1367–82 Soldino. Fine.   4
135 Lucca and Piombino. Felix and Eliz., 1805 5 Fcs. Good.   1
136 Lombardy. Prov. Gov't, 1848 5 Lire. Good.   1
137 Sicily. Ferd. I, 1818 120 Grani. V. good.   1
138 **Medals.** Baden. Fred., 1883 Hd of the Grand Duke and
Grand Duchess *l*., on the 25th anniversary of their marriage.
About perfect. Æ 50.   1
139 Cologne Agricultural Fair, 1865. Column on base with floral
decorations. ℞ 6 line ins. within wrth. Fine. Æ 41.   1
140 Italy. Vic. Em. II, 1878 Upon his death. 54. Wm. II,
Visit to Umberto, 1888. 38. Florence, 1887 Dedication
of Dome. 40. Fine to perfect. All W.m.   3
141 Marguerite of Austria, Jean Sans Peur, Luther, Malines church,
etc. Æ, Brass and W.m. Good to fine, 2 holed. 23 to 60.   10
142 Fractional Currency. All dif., 5 (3), 10 (5), 25 (5), 50c. V.
fine to new and crisp, most of the best. Total, $2.40.   14
143 Confed. States. April 6th, 1863 50c. Fair, a few good.   90

144 **Canada.** Rutherford's, St. John's (3 var.), Halifax, Blakley,
Brown, Gass, Starr & Shannon, Wallace, Purves (unc., red),
Nova Scotia ½ Cents and Cents and 16 varieties of Montreal
Sou Tokens. Good to unc.   28
145 Montreal. Cardinal, Gnaedinger, Phelan, Theriault, 1895 1,
5, 10, 25, 50 Centins, Witness. Fine to unc.   9
146 Pte. Gatineau, Neveu, Quebec, Gagnon, St. Leon (W.m. and
brass), Sorel, Three Rivers, Mascotte, G. N., etc., including
earlier Halfpenny Tokens. Good to unc.   18
147 Duplicates of the three preceding lots. Rutherford's (3) and
early Halfpenny Tokens, including 2 Nova Scotia Half Cents,
also a Communion Token. Good.   13
148 Blakley (3), Gagnon (6), Gass (4), Gnaedinger (6). Gagnon
fine, others unc.   19

149 G. N., 2 var. (5), Purves (4) bright red, Williams, Three Riv-
     ers (2).   Unc.   11

150 St. Leon, 1890.   34.   Montreal Witness.   6.   Unc.   40

151 Communion Tokens.   Hamilton 1846, Lower Settlement, Mait-
     land, Montreal (St. Andrew's and St. Paul's), Noel, Pictou,
     Stewiacke 1830, etc.   Good to v. fine, 1 holed.   10

152 Medals.   Louis XV, 1720.   Bust *r.*   ℞ View of Louisburg
     and its harbor.   LeR.   308.   Perfect.   *Restrike.*   Æ 41.   1

153 Montreal.   Exhibition, 1882 (2), St. John Baptiste Soc., 1884.
     Bust of Duvernay.   Size 35 and 51, both with loop.   Carni-
     val, 1885 (4 var.), '87, Exposition, 1891, '92 (2 var.)   Mostly
     perfect, 2 holed.   Æ gilt, and W.m.   12

154 Congrégation | du | Petit Séminaire | de | Montréal.   Æ 37.
     College of St. Joseph.   W.m. 44.   Irish Cath. Temp. Soc.
     W.m. 44.   LeR. 1309, 1233, 741.   Perfect.   3

155 Hamilton.   1891 Peninsular Saengerfest, Æ and W.m.   Que-
     bec.   Soc. St. John Baptist, 1880 (3 var.) ; St. Anne de
     Beaupre (6), etc.   Æ, brass-plated and W.m.   Mostly per-
     fect ; some odd shapes.   12

156 Buttons.   Earl of Dufferin and Ava, Bank of Montreal, Fire
     Brigade, Canada Militia, Royal Scots of Canada, etc.   Fair
     to perfect.   11

157 Duplicate medals.   St. John Baptiste Soc., large and small ;
     Exp. 1891 (3) ; another with Mr. Breton's name, all holed
     (20) ; Exhibition, 1892 (4).   Fine to perfect.   29

158 U. S. Cents.   1797 to 1857, lacking 9 dates, but includes 1809
     and 1823 (2), 1839, silly head (2).   Early dates poor, later
     ones fair to fine ; 3 holed.   90

159 Rebellion Tokens.   Mass., Rhode Island, Conn., New York,
     State and City.   Fine to unc.   95

160 New Jersey, 7 ; Penna., 17 (9 of Pittsburg) ; West Va., 3 ;
     Michigan, 8 ; Illinois, 9 ; Missouri, 1.   Fine to unc.   45

161 Ohio, representing 26 towns.   A very unusual assortment,
     many unc.   80

162 Indiana, 14 ; Wisconsin, 26 (representing 17 towns), quite as
     important as the preceding.   Mostly unc.   40

163 Others, with merchants' names, without name of town (14).
     Patriotic inscriptions and devices.   Fine to unc.   106

164 Duplicates of War Tokens.   Unassorted ; fine to unc. ; 1 holed.   81

165   Ireland. Jas. I. Gun money. 1689 Shillings, Jan., Sept. (2
      var.), Aug., Nov. 1690 ½ Crowns, May, 2 slightly varying.
      Fair to very good.   7

166   Papal. Paul V, Quattrino ; Leo XII, 1824, Quat. and ½ Bai ;
      Roman Rep., 1849, 1 Bai., siege of Ancona. Fair to good.   4

167   India. Lion l., 5 Cash (?), 1833, '38, '39, '40 ; 20 Cash, 1838,
      with value in English. Good, rare.   6

168   Duplicates of the 5 Cash, dates not well on planchet (3), also
      thick Dumps of native princes, without device (6). Good.   9

169   Money weights. Irish, 1683 ; another with Chas. I, mtd.
      Shop cards, Spiel Marks, Nurembergs, etc. Fair to fine ; 12
      holed, possibly same as issued.   28

170   **Silver coins.** England, Edward I and II. London and
      Canterbury Pennies. Fair to good.   7

171   France. Louis XIII. 1642, 12th Ecu. Good. Papal. Sede
      Vacante, Guilio, 1559, and 2 others, with date indistinct, 1
      plugged. Poor and fair.   4

172   Papal. Leo XIII. 1878 5 Lire, bust facing. Very fine.   1

It is highly probable that the Papal authorities took no part in the minting of
this piece. It is equally certain that its circulation was never permitted.

173   Augsburg. 1642 Thaler. Bust of Ferd. III. ℞ View of the
      city. Very fine.   1

174   Bust of Columbus on concave disk resting on eagle bet. Indian
      and female, who join hands above. By *Johnson*, of Milan.
      A fine bronze medal, in perfect condition. 59.   1

175   France. Exposition of 1867, with bust of Nap. III. Fine.
      Æ 51. Also, various souvenirs of Exp. 1889 ; busts of Dan-
      ton, Robespierre ; views of Eiffel Tower, Bastile, etc. All
      in hard metals, perfect. 23 to 65.   12

---

176   Small Cents. 1857, '58. Unc. '59, '63, '64, '82, '86. Proofs.   7

177   Duplicates of last. 1857, unc. '59, 3 proofs. '63, unc. 5c.,
      1883, without Cents (4) and type of '82, unc.   10

178   1893 Columbian Half Dol. and 2 O. mint Three Cent pieces
      1851. All unc.   3

179   Store Cards. 1789 Motto card. A clock. ℞ Eagle. Fine,
      and one of the best I have seen.   1

180 RICKETTS'S CIRCUS. Garland above, crowned branches below.
     ℞ Arms and crest. Thin planchet, milled edge. Unc., v.
     rare. 28.   1

181 J. & L. Brewster, New York and New Orleans. Fair, v. rare. 26.   1

182 Bondy Brothers & Co. — Belt Manufacturers, New York. ℞
     Plain. Good, very rare. 30.   1

183 (Dr. L.) Feuchtwanger, 2 Cortlandt St. American Silver Com-
     position. ℞ House & Household Furniture, etc. Fine, v.
     rare. 26.   1

184 Wm. Baker & Co. | Up. Chesebrough, Stearns & Co., Cooper
     Union | Check | for books, etc. Espenscheid (℞ Looking
     glass). Foster & Parry (4 var. of planchet), and others
     chiefly of New York, one duplicate. Good to fine, 1 holed.   24

185 Doremus, Suydams & Nixon, 37 & 39 Nassau St., by *B*(ale) &
     S(mith), N. Y. Unc., brass ; rare. 27.   1

186 R. Lovett, Jr. — Philadelphia. ℞ St. George and dragon.
     Unc., in 4 dif. metals. 14½.   4

187 Admit to Wood's Minstrels. "Intrinsic value 25 cents." Very
     fine. 24.   1

188 Various. Black, Electrotyper, 1860 (2 var.) ; Isaac Stevens
     Vanderbilt, 1859 ; R. Flanigan and R. & C. A. Wright, both
     of Phila., etc. Good to fine. All W.m. 14 to 31.   11

189 Foreign Coins, etc. Mexico. A cross *l.*, 1611 *r.*, REI below,
     M̃ ℞ Plain. A rough silver casting. I regret not having
     some information to impart regarding this strange piece,
     further than it has been thought to be a Miner's Token.
     Oblong, silver. 42 x 34.   1

190 1787 2 Reals CS on obv. T(a key) PYE Also a rev. design for
     8 Rls., Iturbide's time. A thin silver shell. Fine.   2

191 1864 Centavo, "Imperio Mexicano." Unc., red, rare in this
     condition.   1

192 1864 5 Ctvos, G. mint. Good. 1867 Peso, M̃ mint, with hd
     of Maximilian. V. fine, but not perfectly centered.   2

193 Durango, ¼ Reals, 1860 and 1866, dif. types. Good.   2

194 Oaxaca. Revolutionary Gen'l Morelos. · M · | · 1 R · | 1813
     ℞ SUD beneath bow and arrow, within floral ornaments.
     Fine, original cast, rare. Æ 21.   1

195 1813 8 Reals. Mon. of Morelos, 8 R. | 1813 ℞ Type of pre-
     ceding. Fine, original cast. Æ 39.   1

196 Tokens of Merchants and Haciendas, principally of towns in
Jalisco. All named in separate envelopes. 7 duplicates.
Mostly good. 20

197 Salvador. 1828 Provisional 2 Reals. Column in sea sep. 2
— R. ℞ Volcano in sea. Good, v. rare. 27. 1

198 Dominica. 2 Bits. D in script, star within a scolloped edge.
℞ Plain. Good, rare. 13½. 1

199 Rep., 1891 5 Ctvs. Æ 25. Hawaii. 1883 Dime. Fine. 2

200 **Medals.** G. A. R. badge and miniature of same, also the
large W.m. medal of same design (size 51). All perfect.
Small heart-shaped shield in red, white and blue, H–M. 88.
Fine. 4

201 McKinley Campaign badge, with portrait; Harrison & Reid,
Tin plate, 1892 ; Herr Alexander, etc. Fine. 5

202 F. Prentice, 26 Pine St., Mining building. ℞ First product |
by | mill process | in the | Pah-Ranagat | etc., 1867. Obv.
edge dent, otherwise fine. Æ 31. 1

203 The Consolidated Kansas City Smelting & Refining Co. to the
American Congress greeting. Two busts conjoined r., below, 1889 ℞ The United Americas — Las Americas Uni-
das — Reciprocity — Commerce. Two figures of Liberty
stdg. Perfect, *rare*. Æ 38. 1

204 1892 CRISTOFORO COLOMBO Bust on concave disc resting on
eagle. America and Europe at sides join hands above.
℞ Allegorical procession of civilization surrounded by genii,
at sunrise, group of Indians show concern at its approach.
Among the finest medals of modern days. Perfect. Bronze
102. 1

205 1892 Another of same design, reduced to size 59. Perfect.
Bronze. 1

206 1892 Bust of Columbus, three caravels sailing in circle. ℞
Spanish and U. S. shields. Ins. in 10 lines. Official medal,
Committee of 100. Perfect. Æ 57. 1

207 Mexico. CAROLUS . II . [*sic*] D . G . HISPN . E . I . REX Bust in
armor facing, by *Gil*. ℞ CUSTODITA CUSTODIT A castle.
Fine, rare. Æ 17. 1

208 Chas. IV, 1789. CAROLUS | IV. | ACCLAMATU | CARTAGVNE| M̃ |
1789 ℞ Castle on island, cwn above, castle and lion alter-
nate around border. Good, very rare. Æ 26½. 1

209 Ferd. VII, 1808 Procl. 2 Rls.   Arms.   ℞ Ins. and date in 6
     lines. V. fine. Æ 27.   1
210 (1821–22) Military medal. Sponsione Triplici ★ etc. Three
     rings looped above two globes, with severed chain. ℞ PRIMA
     EPOCA Loop removed, otherwise fine and rare. Æ 49.   1
211 1862–63 War Medal to the French Soldiers. Head of Nap.
     III, *l.* ℞ EXPEDITION DU MEXIQUE Loop and ring. Very
     fine. Æ 31.   1
212 MAXIMILIANO EMPERADOR   Hd *r.* ℞ AL | MERITO | MILITAR
     Ring and ribbon. Perfect. Æ 33.   1
213 MAXIMILIAN I. IMPERATOR MEHICORUM   Head *r.*, by *Kleeberg.*
     ℞ Birth and death. Angel setd beside tomb. Fon. 6707.
     Nearly perfect, very rare. W.m. 41.   1
214 Oaxaca. Ferd. VII, 1809. Mil. bust *l.* *Ex.* PROREGE ARCH |
     LIZANA ℞ SANCTÆ ANTEQUERENSE (Oaxaca). Minerva
     setd *l.* Betts Cat. 647. Fine. Æ 52 x 62.   1
215 Pasquaro. Ferd. VII, 1808. Cwnd arms. ℞ PROCLAMADO |
     EN PASQUARO etc. Betts Cat. 881. *Restrike.* Perfect. Æ 40. 1
216 Puebla. 1833, War Medal. EL GOBIERNO DE LA UNION A LOS
     HEROICOS etc. ℞ LA FEDERATION TRIUNFANT etc. Large
     die-projecting loop. Betts Cat. 652. Fine. Æ 30 x 40.   1
217 Queretaro. Ferd. VII, 1808. Cwnd arms. ℞ PROCLAMADO |
     EN QUERETARO | etc., in 5 lines. Perfect. *Restrike.* Æ 33
     (unusual size). San Luis Potosi. 1828 Mexico Libre. In-
     dian princess setd. Holed, fine. Æ 29.   2
218 San Mateo de Huichapan. Ferd. VII, 1809. Cwnd arms. ℞
     PROCLAMADO | EN S. MATEO DE | HUICHAPAN | etc., in 6 lines.
     Restrike. Perfect, originals unknown, very rare. Æ 36.   1
219 Santiago de Tuxtla. Ferd. VII, 1809. Cwnd arms. ℞ PRO-
     CLAMADO | EN LA VILLA DE | SANTIAGO TUXTLA | etc., in 8
     lines. *Restrike.* Perfect. Æ 40.   1
220 Sombrerete. Chas. IV, 1791. Cwnd arms, border of dots.
     ℞ JURA ＊ DE ＊ SOMBRERETE ＊ ANO ＊ DE ＊ Rock within
     circle, on pedestal. *Restrikes.* Perfect. Æ sizes 32, 37. 2
221 Zamora. Ferd. VII, 1808. Cwnd arms, floral border. ℞
     PROCLAMADO EN LA VILLA etc. In field, 6 line ins. *Restrike.*
     Perfect. Æ 40.   1
222 — Ferd. VII, 1808. Same design as last. *Restrike.* Per-
     fect. Æ 32.   1

223 Chiapas. Augustin, 1822, Procl. Real. Holed, fine. 20.
Guatemala. Chas. III, 1760, Procl. ½ Real. Holed, good.
16½ and a brass Token with Lib. cap in rays. Fine. 21. 3

224 Cadiz. Ferd. VII, 1816. Head *r.* ℞ Mars and Indian hold
open book resting on two globes, ins. CONSTI | TUCI | ON |
POLITI | CA — etc. Fine, but small piece restored nearly
obliterates date. Æ 56. Another of same date. Hercules
standing bet. pillars restrains two lions. Perfect. Æ 34. 2

----

225 Hard Times Tokens. 1834 "For the Constitution Hurra !"
Ship sailing *l.* Low 2. Obv. good, rev. barely fair. 1

226 1834 Boar running *l.* ℞ Bust of Jackson. Unc., one partly
bright. Rev. die of one is slightly cracked, a noticeable fea-
ture is a "wart" on Jackson's chin. L. 4. 2

227 Another, from same dies as last, in brass. L. 5. V. good, rare. 1

228 Same type as last two preceding. Jackson has *very* broad
shoulders. L. 6. Very fine. 1

229 Jackson walking with sword and money bags. "A plain sys-
tem." L. 8. V. fine. Bucklin, West Troy. L. 13. Fair. 2

230 Female head *r.* ins. TROY ℞ A screw-bolt. Machine shop,
etc. L. 11. Good, very rare. 1

231 Jackson in treasure chest. ℞ Donkey stdg *l.* Six spaces on
end of chest are without horizontal lines ; another has four
unfilled ; a third with all spaces filled. L. 16. Unc., 2 partly
bright. 3

232 Another from same dies as last, in brass, all spaces in treasure
chest filled. L. 17. Fine. 1

233 Jackson in treasure chest, type of the preceding, donkey has
larger and ill-shaped body. L. 18. Fine. 1

234 Merchants Exchange. ℞ Not one Cent, etc. With and without dash below Cent. Also the new Exchange. L. 19, 21,
22. Good to fine. 3

235 1837 Turtle carrying safe. ℞ Jackass running *l.* The "short
ground " variety. L. 23. Good, very rare. 1

236 Varieties of type of last. "Experiment " 2, " Financiering " 1.
L. 24, 25, 26. Unc., all partly bright. 3

237 1837 Female hd *l.*, laureated, 13 stars. ℞ Not | one | Cent |
etc. Wreath. L. 27. Good, rev. scratched, rare. 1

238   1837 Another, same general type, smaller and ill-shaped head,
      15 stars, 2 of the very small.   L. 28.   Nearly fine, difficult
      to excel, rare.   1

239   1837 Another, sim., with head inscribed UNITED   Largest
      date in the series.   L. 29.   Fine, some corrosion on obv.,
      rare.   1

240   1837 Another, head laur., 6 stars on *l.* (the Dayton head), L.
      34 ; and 7 stars *l.*, L. 37 ; a still dif. head (with rev. same
      as 37), L. 38 ; and a new rev., L. 39.   Good to unc., partly
      bright.   4

241   1837 Ugly female head *l.*, masculine features, same as used
      on Crossman and Maycock's cards.   L. 35.   Good, rare.   1

242   1837 Female head *l.*, laur.   End of scroll terminates under
      second U in UNUM, with 6 differing revs.   Mint Drop, May
      10th, etc.   L. 40, 41, 42, 43, 44, 45.   Good to v. fine.   6

243   1837 Jackson in treasure chest.   ℞ Wrecked ship, and Phoenix
      rising from flames, with 4 dif. revs.   L. 49, 50, 51, 52, 53.
      Fine to unc.   5

244   1837 " Half Cent worth of pure copper " Dayton's card, also
      Crossman's, 2 var., and Maycock's.   L. 54, 61, 62, 63, 65.
      Fine.   5

245   " A friend to the Constitution."   A steer *r.*   ℞ A ship.   L. 56.
      Good, dent obv. and rev., rare.   1

246   Others.   Centre Market 2 var., Cards of Jarvis 2 var., Riker,
      Sweet and Deveau.   L. 66, 67, 68, 69, 70, 72, 74.   Good to
      fine, 3 are very uncommon.   7

247   1837 Arms of New York, 3 Cents, and eagle on serpent, 1 Cent,
      both Feuchtwanger metal; slave kneeling and 1838 Loco
      Foco head.   L. 75, 78, 79, 80.   Good to fine.   4

248   " The sober second thoughts " etc.   Bust of Van Buren.   ℞
      Eagle with scroll above safe.   L. 81.   Gd, holed as all are.   1

249   1841 Webster — Credit Current.   Ship, 3 var. with varying
      revs., also female head with leaves in place of stars, with 3
      revs.   L. 84, 85, 86, 88, 90, 92, 93, 94.   1 good, others fine
      to unc., partly bright.   8

250   1841 Ship without jib, 4 stays from foremast to bowsprit.   ℞
      Wrecked ship.   L. 89.   V. fine, rare.   1

251   1841 Ship, leaves in place of stars.   ℞ Female head *l.*   L. 91.
      Good, edge dent, rare.   1

252   Curiosities of the series. L. 6, Jackson with broad shoulders. ℞ Incuse impression of same. Holed. L. 34, Dayton head, with incuse of same on rev. L. 35, Ugly head, incuse impression, with correct rev. in relief.   3

253   Duplicates of Hard Times Tokens. L. 4 (12), 6 (4), 8 (3), 13, 16 (12), 18 (3), 19, 21 (7), 22, 24, 25 and 26 (10 each), 28, 29, 34 (3), 35 (2), 39 (7), 40, 42 (2). Many good to fine.   100

254   Others. L. 42 (2), 44 (2), 45, 49, 50 (3), 51 (7), 52 (2), 53 (10), 54 (10), 62 (2), 63 (2), 65 (3), 66 (2), 67 (7), 69 (3), 70 (2), 74, 78 (10), 79 (3), 80, 84, 86 and 88 (2 each), 90 (8), 92 (5), 93, 94 (5). Many good to fine.   100

255   Store Cards, prior to 1861. Attleboro, Boston, Taunton, New Haven, Buffalo, Oswego, Rochester, Saratoga Springs, Syracuse, Troy, Utica. Mostly good to unc.   20

256   New York City, Chesebrough, Bollenhagen, Crystal Palace, Doremus & Nixon, Tredwell, Kissam & Co., C. & I. D. Wolfe, etc. Mostly good to fine.   40

257   Glassboro, Howell Works Garden, C. & D. Canal 1825, Phila. (13), Pittsburg, Detroit, Grand Rapids, Milwaukee, Chicago, etc. (1 dated 1845). Many good to unc.   33

258   St. Louis, Cinn., Louisville, Memphis, Nashville, Norfolk, Petersburg, Charleston, Vicksburg, New Orleans, San Francisco. Good to unc.   28

259   Others, various, mostly in W.m., some small and early, including Soulsby and Randall, both Balto. Mostly good to fine, 2 holed.   25

260   Others. Rubber (5), Not One Cent, 1855 (4), Rebellion Tokens, etc. Fair to good, 4 holed.   19

261   Duplicates of Store Cards, Omnibus, Mineral Water Tickets, etc., including 10 in rubber. 13 holed, prob. as issued, many good to unc.   104

262   Calendars, 1749, '67, '76, '78, 1803, all Birmingham make, 1853 London, '53 (2), '54, '55 (3), New York City, Ohio, Ill. 2 in W.m., others brass. 1 holed, mostly fine. 34 to 44.   12

263   U. S. Cents. 1817 (4), '21 (25), '23 (6), '37 (10), '38 (10). The last year good to fine, others poor and fair.   55

264   1821 Poor and fair (25), '53 Very good (13), '55 Straight 55, unc., red, slight blemishes (19).   57

265   1821 Very fair to nearly good.   39

266   1838 Fine and very fine (18), '55 Straight 55, unc., red, slight
      blemishes (25), '56 Italic 5, mostly v. fine (18).   61

267   1855 Unc., red, slight blemishes, '56 Italic 5, v. fine to unc.
      mostly, partly bright (25 each).   50

268   1855 Straight 55. Unc., bright red, free from stains, nearly
      perfect.   50

269   1855 Another lot, quite as last.   48

270   1855 Another, the equal of either of the preceding.   64

271   Others of same date. Unc., red, mostly with slight spots or
      stains.   116

272   Elephant, "God preserve London." Much nicked.   1787
      Fugio. Unc. Washington, Lib. & Security Penny. West
      Troy, L. 13, etc. Fair to v. good.   14

273   **Medals.** *Bronze.* Allston, Wash., 1847, Am. Art Union.
      Fine. 64.   1

274   Beecher, Hy Ward. Head *r.* ℞ Dates of birth and death.
      V. fine. 76.   1

275   Columbus, Chris. Large bust, by *Johnson*, of Milan. Chicago,
      1893. Perfect. 59.   1

276   Columbus in stern of vessel, by *Christensen*, Copenhagen. Chi-
      cago Exposition. About perfect. 65.   1

277   Columbus, bust facing, with hat, by *Massonnet*, of Paris. Chi-
      cago Exp. Æ gilt, 51. About perfect.   1

278   Ericsson, J. 1889, his death. ℞ The famous Monitor. By
      Ahlborn. Perfect. 31.   1

279   Fillmore, M. 1850, Pres. U. S. ℞ Indian and soldier before
      U. S. flag. Fine. 76.   1

280   Franklin and Montyon. 1833, Busts conjoined. 42. Grant,
      U. S. Bust *r.* ℞ Tomb, mil. trophy. 37½. Abt per-
      fect.   2

281   Grant, U. S. 1868, Bust *l.*, by *Bovey.* ℞ I intend to fight it
      out, etc. About perfect. 60.   1

282   — Head *r.*, 1869, Oceans united. ℞ "Every mountain shall
      be made low," train of cars approaching ocean. Perfect. 46.   1

283   Hosack, D. Head *r.* ℞ Arts and Science. Perfect. 34.   1

284   Howard, J. E. 1781, Battle of Cowpens. "Comitia Ameri-
      cana." Betts 595. V. fine. 46.   1

285   Kelly, John. 1868, Late Tammany Hall Leader. Head *r.*,
      by *Sigel.* New York City School medal. V. fine, rare. 63.   1

286 Macdonough, Tho. Bust *r.*, by *Furst.* ℞ Scene of his victory on Lake Champlain. Nearly perfect. 65. 1

287 Madison, J. 1809, Pres. U. S. Bust *l.* ℞ Peace and Friendship, hands joined, pipe and tomahawk. V. fine. 63. 1

288 Washington, Geo. 1797, Pres. Unit. Sta. Bust *r.* ℞ Commiss. Resigned, etc. Fine. 41. 1

289 — Another, a bronzed proof, nearly perfect. 41. 1

290 — Another, a late impression, thick planchet. Perfect. 41. 1

291 — Bust *r.*, by *Paquet.* ℞ Wash. Cabinet of Medals inaugurated at United States Mint, February 22, 1860. Fine, edge dent. 60. 1

292 — Bust *l.*, by *Saint Gaudens.* 1889 Centennial of inauguration at New York. An artistic original cast, in fine preservation. 113. 1

293 1776 Continental C'y Seal. *Res.* 1846 Medal for Gallantry and Humanity. Balloon City of N. Y. G. A. R. Badge and Harrison & Morton inauguration, 1889. Fine. 5

294 1870 Annual Assay. Moneta stdg. Perfect. *Aluminum.* 34. 1

295 1871 Annual Assay. Archimedes stdg. Perfect. 33. 1

296 1876 Centennial at Phila. Busts of Victoria, McMahon, Wilhelm and Pius IX. " See how we prosper." About perfect. 44. 4

297 1877 Annual Assay. Type as 295. 1

298 1880 Worcester Continentals, Souvenir. 1891 Inter-state Encampment, Patriarchs Militant, I. O. O. F., Syracuse, others undated, " In God we trust," 3 links, " Union is the bond of Society," hands joined. 1 in brass, 3 are about perfect ; a very uncommon lot. 38 to 48. 4

299 Various small medals. Wash., Jackson, Harrison, Taylor, Lincoln, Grant, etc. 9 holed as issued, some in brass, many good to perfect. 19

300 Others. Asbury, Moody, Wesley, College of N. Y., Delta Psi, Richmond Hill House, etc. 6 holed as issued, some in brass, many fine to perfect. 18

301 White Metal Medals. Wash., Clay, Douglas, Lincoln, Scott, Johnson, Grant, Ericsson, etc. Including N. Y. Reservoir 1842, Springfield 1883 " Bycicle " (and " Bicycle " said to be unique) Tournament. Good to perfect, 10 holed. 18 to 51. 30

302 **Uncirculated Sets.** Brazil. Rep., 1889 20, 40 Reis, Æ ;
     100, 200 do., nickel ; 500, 1000 do., Æ, and Dom Pedro
     2000 do.   7
303 British East Africa Co. Mombasa, 1888 ¼ Anna, Æ ; 2 do.
     and ¼, ½ and 1 Rupee, Æ.   5
304 — Another set as last.   5
305 — 3 more sets.   15
306 — 4 more sets.   20
307 Dominica. 1891 5, 10 Ctmos., Æ ; 50 do. and 1, 5 Francos.   5
308 — Another set as last.   5
309 — 2 more sets.   10
310 — 3 more sets.   15
311 — 5 more sets, lacking the copper pieces.   15
312 German East Africa. 1891–92 ¼ Anna, Æ ; ¼, ½ and 1 Rupee, Æ.   4
313 — Another set as last, with the Rupee in proof, as are also
     those in the following sets.   4
314 — 3 more sets.   12
315 — 3 more sets.   12
316 — 4 more sets.   16
317 Qwang-tung (China). 3.6 Candareens, 7.2 do., 1 Mace 4.4
     Can., 6 Mace 6 Can., 7 Mace 2 Can. 5c. to $1 size.   5
318 — Another set as last.   5
319 — 2 more sets.   10
320 South African Rep. 1892 3, 6d., 1, 2 and 2½ Shil., all with
     bust of Paul Kruger. Proofs.   5
321 — Another set as last.   5
322 — 2 more sets.   10
323 — 2 more sets.   10
324 **Various Silver Coins.** Travancore. Chuckrum. The
     Emperor setd. ℞ Native inscription. Fine. Size 10.   25
325 — Another lot.   50
326 — Another lot.   100
327 — The letter J ? 12 dots behind, with rev. as last. Fine. 10. 25
328 — Others as last.   50
329 — Another lot.   100
330 *Ancient.* Antiochia. Potin tetradrachms (part silver). Nero,
     Galba, Vespasian, Trajan, Hadrian and Caracalla, all with
     Emperor's head. Each fully described in separate envelope.
     Fair to about good.   6

331   Another, sim., lacking Hadrian.   5
332   Others. Poor to fair. Nero (10), Vespasian (5), Trajan (7),
      Caracalla (2). Many varieties.   24
333   Others as last. Nero (11), Vespasian (5), Trajan (6).   22
334   Others. Nero (11), Vespasian (5), Trajan (7).   23
335   **Silver Medals.** Mexico. 1797 Church Medal. Statue of
      Remedios. Loop. 28 x 34. Ferd. VII, 1808 Procl. Arms.
      ℞ 6 line ins., wrth. 27. Fine.   2
336   1822 Inauguration | de Agustin, etc. in 5 lines. ℞ Eagle on
      cactus. Fine. 34. Also Proclamation Reals of Guatemala
      and S. Salvador. Both holed, good and fair.   3
337   1869 School Medal. ℞ Al | talento | y la | aplicacion. V.
      fine. 45½.   1
338   Guadalaxara. Liceo | de | Varones, and The Seminary.
      Bene | Merenti. Very fine. 35½.   2
339   Jalisco. 1873 Head of Gen'l Corona r. ℞ POR LA MONHO-
      NERA. Given to participants in battle of Mohonera. Per-
      fect. 35.   1
340   — State arms. ℞ Premio | a la | instruccion. Fine.
      37.   1
341   Cayenne. Compagnie de | la · Cayenne | Francaise. Negro
      beside his cabin at seaside. ℞ Agriculture | et | Commerce.
      Perfect. *Restrike.* Octagonal, 33½.   1
342   Amsterdam. 1770 Lutheran Alms House. 1784 Capt. De
      Roth's Medal and other Dutch Medalets and Jetons, 1585,
      1745, '51, '85, etc. 23 to 39. Good to fine.   7
343   Others of Harlem, Leyden, Utrecht, etc., 1617, 1669, 1775 and
      others undated. Good to fine. 27 to 33.   7
344   Middleburg. 1741 New Lutheran Church. Light setd beside
      structure holds open book, plumb and level. Van Loon,
      Supl. 163. Fine. 49.   1
345   France. Louis XIV, Neptune in car. Louis XV, Rochelle
      Chamber of Commerce (2 var.). The French Academy,
      "To Immortality." Louis XVI, Court Procurers, "We get
      ready the Judicial Plow." Jetons, all with bust. Good to
      fine. 27 to 31.   5
346   Others, later. Bonaparte | op | St. Helena. Napoleon setd
      on rock. Bordeaux, Lyons (2), Poitiers, Rouen (2), etc.
      Good to perfect, brilliant, most of the best. 27 to 31.   8

347   Octagonal Jetons, 1791, 1822, etc.   Bank of France, Caisse
       Patriotique, Messageries Imperiales, etc.   Fine to perfect.
       Octagonal.   33 to 36.   7
348   Others.   Courtiers de Commerce, Chamber de Commerce,
       Lyons and Rouen, etc., one with bust of Louis XVIII.   Gd
       to perfect.   Octagonal.   32 to 36.   7
349   France.   Society of Medicine, Feby 10th, 1868 "Science Verite
       Justice."   Nearly perfect.   37.   1
350   Hamburg.   In remembrance of John Parish's Fifty years' stay,
       etc., 1756–1806.   V. fine.   40.   1
351   Germany.   Wm. II, 1890 Acquisition of the island of Heligo-
       land.   Proof, slight tarnish.   38.   1
352   Moltke, Field Marshal.   His hd r.   In memory of National
       holiday upon his 90th birthday, Oct. 26th, 1890.   About per-
       fect.   35.   1
353   Stuttgart.   1875 Shooting Festival.   City arms.   ℞ Germania
       standing.   About perfect.   41.   1
354   Jonathan and David shaking hands.   WAS · DU · UND · ICH ·
       MIT EINAN : GER : HAB :   Very good, loop removed.   45.   1
355   Vienna.   1845 Opening of railroad, Aug. 20th.   View of tun-
       nel, locomotive entering.   Nearly perfect.   44.   1
356   Jetons and Medalets.   Coronation, New Year, Bribery, etc.
       17th to 19th century.   Good to fine.   20 to 28.   9
357   Another asst. and similar in character, one in lozenge form
       dated 1609.   Good to fine, 2 have loops removed.   21 to 28. 8
358   Others, of Russia, 1774, 1790, 1791.   Fine.   21 to 23.   3
359   La Crimea.   1855 Turkish-Crimea.   War Medal.   Holed,
       with ring and ribbon.   Fine.   37.   1
360   Sweden.   Gust. Adolph., 1631 Bust r.   ℞ Lion with sword
       and buckler.   DEO · ET · VICTRICIBVS · ARMIS   War Medal.
       Holed, with ring, good, rare.   Elliptical, 31 x 40.   1
361   1632 Bust in ornate ellipse.   ℞ Hand holds sword erect, date
       of birth and death.   Fine, light scratches on obv.   44.   1
362   Chas. X, 1654–60 ISTO CREVIMVS ENSE.   3 cwns above sword
       ptd l.   ℞ Date of birth, coronation and death.   Fine.   32. 1
363   Chas. XI.   Head r.   ℞ Head of Ulrica Eleonora his wife,
       mother of Chas. XII.   Fine.   29.   1
364   Gust. Adolph. 1772, Chas. XIV John 1818, Chas. XV 1860.
       All bust r.   Last 2 coronation.   V. fine, 2 are bril.   30, 31. 3

365 Sirmoor, India. 1886 BIR EIKRAM SINGH OF SIRMOOR Arms
supported by lion; crest, an elephant. Persian inscription
in rev. field. V. fine, native work, rare. 41½.   1

PORTRAIT MEDALS IN BRONZE.
All with bust.

366 **Rulers.** Belgium. Leop. I, 1831 Declaration of his policy.
Louise Marie d'Orleans, his wife, upon her death, 1850.
Fine. 50.   2

367 Leop. I, Mil. bust *l.*, by *Braemt.* ℞ Plain. Fine. 68. 1853
Leop., Duke of Brabant, 18th birthday. About perfect. 51.   2

368 Leop., Duke; head *r.* ℞ Wreath, plain field, light nicks. 58.
Another, upon his marriage to Maria of Aust., 1853. Their
heads conjoined *l.* Nearly perfect. 59.   2

369 Another, for the same occasion, by *Wiener*, heads conjoined *l.*
℞ Female stdg, lion *l.*, burning altar *r.* About perfect.   1

370 Leop. I, 1856 Laying of first stone of "Kathendyke." About
perfect. 64. Also Phil., Duke of Brabant. Exposition,
1854. Fine. 52.   2

371 Leop. I, and Wm. III of Netherlands, on their meeting at
Liege, Oct. 19th, 1861. Their heads conjoined *l.* Fine,
some nicks. 70.   1

372 Another, upon their meeting at Brussels, May 20th, 1884.
Their heads *l.*, by *Fisch.* Perfect. 70.   1

373 Netherlands. Wm. I, 1838 Approval and proclamation of
code for Belgium. V. fine, nearly perfect. 65.   1

374 France. Louis XVI, 1787 Judicial Benefit Ass'n. Fine. 70.
Chas. X, Upon his accession, 1825. Nearly perfect. 51.   2

375 L. Philippe, 1845 Viaduct of Dinan. V. fine. 68. Nap. III,
1852 Protection of sailors' orphan children. V. fine. 60.   2

376 Denmark. Chris. VIII, 1840 25th anniversary of his marriage to Caroline. Their heads conjoined *r.* V. fine. 48.   1

377 Prussia. Fred. II, 1840 Statue to Fred. the Great. Fine,
some light nicks. 50. Modena. Francis IV, 1814 Resto-
ration of the City. Fine. 42.   2

378 Germany. Frederick, upon his death, June 15th, 1888. Fine
bust *r.*, by *Lauer.* Perfect. 70.   1

379 Wm. II, 1889 Upon his visit to England. Naval review. V.
fine. 60.   1

380 Papal.   Pius IX, 1863 Congress in his honor at Malines. Fine.
     60.   Naples and Sicily.   Fran. I and Eliz., 1825 Accession.
     Fine. 61.   2
381 **Eminent Persons.** Albarea, J. L., 1881 Visited inundation
     at Seville. Nearly perfect. 51.   Alfieri, V., *It.* Dramatist.
     Ariosto, Poet and Dramatist. Last 2 belong to Series Num.
     About perfect. 41.   3
382 Anspach, J., 1872 Burgomaster of Brussels. Fine, a few nicks.
     66.   Bara, J., *Belg.* Representative. Fine. 60.   2
383 Bartakovics, A., 1865 Archb. of Agram. About perfect. 44.
     Belmas, L., 1757–1841 Bishop of Cambray. V. fine. 54.   2
384 Beethoven, von, L., Head *r.*, without legend, beaded border.
     ℞ Austrian arms, dates of birth and death. A finely exe-
     cuted medal, in light bronze. Perfect. 50.   1
385 Berry, C. F., Duke de, Assassinated in Paris, 1820. V. fine.
     56.   Cimarosa, D., *It.* Composer (Ser. Num.).   Clarion, L.
     de La Tude, *Fr.* Actress, d. 1803. V. fair. 44.   3
386 Corneille, P., *Fr.* Dramatist, d. 1684 (Ser. Num.). Fine. De-
     saugiers, M. A., *Fr.* Song-writer and Dramatist. Good. 42.
     Gluysenaar, J. P., *Belg.* Architect. V. fine. 68.   3
387 Jehotte, L., *Belg.* Sculptor, by the Liege Soc'y, 1851. Fine,
     some nicks. 68.   Maffei, F. S., *It.* Dramatist, d. 1755. Fine.
     55.   2
388 Kemble, J. P., *Eng.* Tragedian, d. 1823, by *Hancock.* Fine. 53. 1
389 Liszt, F. Head *r.*, by *Geerts*, without legend. ℞ A | Franz
     Liszt | Souvenir | du 29 Mai 1881 | les Artistes Musiciens |
     de | Bruxelles. About perfect. 65.   1
390 Marcellis, C. Covering of the Bourse, at Antwerp, 1850–54.
     Fine. 60.   Moliere, P., *Fr.* Dramatist, d. 1673. V. fine. 57. 2
391 Marchionnia, Carolotta, 1822 Scenic Artist in Bologna. Mo-
     zart, W., *Ger.* Composer, d. 1791.   Piccini, N., *It.* Composer,
     d. 1800. Rameau, J. P., *Fr.* Violinist and Composer, d. 1764.
     Last 3 Ser. Num. All fine. 43, 41.   4
392 Rogier, C., 1858 *Belg.* Minister of the Interior. Fine, some
     nicks. 68.   Verhaegen, P. T., Pres. *Belg.* Chamber of Rep-
     resentatives. Fine, a few nicks. 68.   2
393 Sacchini, A., *It.* Composer, d. 1786. Ser. Num. Tegner, E.,
     Swed., Lyric Poet, d. 1846. 38. Vega, L. de, *Sp.* Poet and
     Dramatist, d. 1635. Ser. Num. All v. fine.   3

394 Schiller, F., *Ger*. Poet and Dramatist, d. 1805. Ser. Num.
Another, head *l.*, by *Kullrich*, Cent'l of his birth, 1859. 38.
Both perfect. 2

395 *In Silver*. Francis, Jos., 1879 Dbl Gulden on 25th Marriage
anniversary. Head of Emperor and Empress. V. fine. 1

396 Mendelssohn, Moses. Bust *l*. ℞ PHAEDON Butterfly on
skull. *Ex.* NATUS | MDCCXXIX About fine. 43. 1

MASONIC MEDALS.

397 **Silver.** Guadalajara — Eureka N · 88 in centre of 5-ptd star.
☒ — R — A — A — E. ℞ Plain. M. 967. Fine. 55. 1

398 Latomia (the genius of Masonry) standing. ℞ G in radiant
triangle. Legends in the quadrate cypher. M. 27. About
fine. 46. Struck in 1825 by the Netherlands Grand Lodge
on the marriage of Prince Frederic, their G. M. 1

399 Grand Orient of France. Juncti Roborantur. Fasces. ℞
Omnibus Unus. Sun in triangle. M. 162. Fine. 30. 1

400 Archimedes setd *r.* LOGE ARCHIMEDES | etc. ℞ GEGRUNDET |
DEN 12 AUGUST | 1802. M. 351. Loop removed, a few
nicks. 36. 1

401 WIELAND Bust *l*. ℞ Sphinx *l*. holds triangle within wreath.
On his 80th birthday by the Lodge Amalia, Weimar, 1812.
M. 418. Fine, rare. 1

402 **Bronze.** Baltimore. Maryland Commandery 100th Anniversary 1890. Proof. 37. 1

403 — Grand Masonic Fair 1890, Grand Lodge of Maryland.
Proof. 37. 1

404 Erie. 1891, 38th Conclave Grand Commandery of Penna.
Proof. 37. 1

405 New York. Old Masonic Hall, 1827–56, with 2 dif. reverses.
Each in Æ and brass. Perfect. 31. 4

406 — Masonic Temple, 1875. ℞ Old Masonic Hall. Æ and
brass; also Masonic altar. *Mules.* Perfect. 31. 3

407 Phila. 1886, Kadosh, St. Alban's, Corinthian and Kensington
Commanderies. ℞ Pilgrimage of the St. Louis Club. Proof.
35. 1

408 St. Louis. 1886, Triennial Conclave, Masonic Knights Tem-
plar. Proof. 37½. 1

409 Utica. Dedication of the Asylum, James Ten Eyck, G. M.
     Perfect. 40.   1
410 Washington. 1889, City of Mexico Club, K. T., of Phila.
     Proof. 37½.   1
411 — 1889, 24th Triennial Conclave, Knights Templars. Proof.
     37½.   1
412 Various U. S. Masonic Medalets. Lake City Lodge. 3 with
     bust of Washington, etc. Fine to perfect, 2 holed. 18 to
     27.   9
413 Batavia. 1856–58, DE STER IN HET OOSTEN | TE | BATAVIA.
     The front of a temple, by *Massonnet.* M. 689. Scarce ;
     proof. 41.   1
414 Belgium. LEOPOLD DE SAXE COBURG etc. Head of Leop. *r.*
     bet. 2 inverted torches. ℞ GR.·. OR.·. DE BELGIQUE. A 6-
     pointed star. Mortuary. M. 40. Fine. 30.   1
415 — Bust of Stassart *l.* ℞ LES LIBERAUX BELGES | etc., in 14
     lines. M. note p. 80. Nearly perfect. 50.   1
416 — Phoenix rising. RESURGENS TENEBRAS etc. ℞ G on 5-ptd
     star. AD MAJOREM DEI GLORIAM etc., in 8 lines. M. 188.
     Nearly perfect. 45.   1
417 La Mac.·. Vivra ♀ etc. Serpent biting a file. ℞ " The Ma-
     sonic Sermon " in *forty-one* lines. M. 191. Good. 50.   1
418 Nantes. A LA GL.·. DU GRA.·. etc. ℞ Assiduite | travail | de-
     vouement M. 806. Proof. 41.   1
419 Commandeurs du Mont Thabor. Level within wrth. M. 149.
     Fine. O.·. de Gray. Eye within triangle on large radiation.
     M. 801. And LA L.·. | FRATERNIDAD etc. M. 680. The
     last 2 proofs. 31, 41, 37.   3
420 Rendsburg. North Star Lodge, on 8-pointed flaming gilt star
     set with square green stone in centre, 52 x 59 bet. pts ; also,
     Odd Fellows, Topeka, Kas., 1890 ; Knights of Pythias, Mil-
     waukee, 1890, both 35. Perfect.   3
421 Netherlands. Bruderschaft medal in memory of Legate Joh.
     Monnihoff, 1787.· Two right hands joined. ℞ A belt, wound
     and tightened around rod. V. L. supplement, 689. About
     perfect. 63.   1
422 **White Metal.** Maryland Commandery, 1890, Balto. ; Ma-
     sonic Fair, Batavia, O.·. De Gray.·. New Brunswick, Canada,
     etc. Perfect.   8

423 Others. Nantes; Triennial Conclave, St. Louis, 1886 ; City of Mexico Club ; K. T. of Phila., 24th Triennial Conclave, Wash., 1889 ; La L.·. Fraternidad, etc. Perfect. 9

A CITY CONSIGNMENT.

424 **Ancient.** Macedonia. Phil. III, B. C. 324–317. Drachm. Good. 16. 1

425 Antonia. Marcus Antonius, head of Victory ; another, Lituus, præfericulum and raven. Quinarii. Fair and good, the latter holed. 2

426 Julius Caesar. His head *r.* ℞ L · BVCA Denarius. Good ; portrait fine. 1

427 A different head of Caesar, veiled. ℞ P . SEPVLLIVS . MACER . Denarius. Good. 1

428 Augustus, B. C. 27, A. D. 14. Good. Nero, A. D. 54–68. Obv. good, rev. fair. Both with head in profile *r.* Denarii. 2

429 **Judaea.** Lepton or Widows' Mites. John Hyrcanus I, B. C. 135–106. Good. 1

430 Alex. Jannaeus, B. C. 105–78 ; Augustus, B. C. 27, A. D. 14. Poor and fair. 2

431 Herod Agrippa, A. D. 37–44 ; Claudius, 41–54 ; Nero, 54–68. Poor and fair. 3

432 Simon Nasi, A. D. 67–68. Fine. 1

433 **Colonial.** Massachusetts. 1652 Pine-tree Shilling. Large planchet. (M)ASA(C)HVSETS IN Fair. Tree well defined, rev. good. 30. 1

434 Another. Stumpy tree, fewer branches, much worn through centre, obliterating top of tree and several letters ; rev. good, clipped to centre of letters W.EN. 29. 1

435 Another, same var. The circumference clipped to centre of legend, otherwise fair, date plain. 24. 1

436 Another. Tree with branches less perpendicular, heavy root with stems ; piece out of edge bet. A and N Barely fair. 29. 1

437 Another. Small planchet. Good, though some letters on rev. are much worn. 24. 1

438 Another. Similar, though tree differs ; slightly clipped. V. fair. 23. 1

439 1652 Pine-tree Sixpence. Fair, date strong, small pin-hole, clipped. 18. 1

440 New York. 1795 Talbot, Allum & Lee. Cent. Abt unc.
      Dark olive.   1
441 San Francisco. THURNAUER & ZINN — S. FRANCISCO. In field,
      a large C. ℞ Head with coronet ins. Liberty, below COMP.
      S. MARKE. Fine, and I believe unpublished, period about
      1856–60. Brass. 27.   1
442 **The U. S. Mint Series.** Half Cent, 1793. Very good ; a
      light olive.   1
443 1856 Sharp proof ; not in full brilliancy.   1
443a Cents. 1793 Chain of 15 links. AMERICA. Good.   1
443b 1794 Hays, No. 11. Very fine, a few light nicks.   1
444 1804 Only last two figures of date show, otherwise fair.   1
445 1804 Much worn, but date still well established.   1
446 1809 A strong impression, fine corrosion. Very good.   1
447 Small Cents. 1858, '59, '60, '63, '80, '97. Unc. ; all brilliant
      excepting '63.   6
448 Two Cents. 1864 to 1871. Unc., red.   8
448a 1873 Proof ; rarest of series.   1
449 Three Cents. 1852, '53, '57, '59, '61. Unc.   5
450 Nickel Three Cents. 1877 Proof ; rarest of series.   1
451 Half Dimes. 1797 Poor ; date good.   1
452 1800 Nearly fine.   1
453 1805 Very good, extremely rare.   1
454 1846 Good, rare.   1
454a Nickel Five Cents. 1877 Proof ; rarest of series.   1
455 Dimes. 1798, 1805, '07, '11, '20, '21 (large and small date),
      '23, '24, '25, '27, '29. Poor to good. Mostly v. fair.   12
456 1822 Very fair, rare.   1
457 Twenty Cents. 1877 Proof. Rare.   1
458 1878 Proof. Rare.   1
459 Quarter Dols. 1804 Fair, holed through head. Rare.   1
460 1806 over '05. Good.   1
461 1807 Good.   1
462 1821 Very good.   1
462a 1893 Isabella. Issued under the auspices of the Board of
      Lady Managers, Columbian Exposition.   1
463 Half Dols. 1795 Very good.   1
464 1801 Very good, rare.   1
465 1802 Very good, rare.   1

466	1803 Very good.	1
467	1852 Extremely fine ; only slightest marks of circulation ; rare.	1
468	Dollars. 1795 Flowing hair. Very good, nearly fine.	1
469	1798 Large eagle, close date. Very good.	1
470	1798 Large eagle, wide date. Very good.	1
471	1799 Very fine.	1
472	1800 Nearly fine.	1
473	1802 Very good.	1
474	1803 Large 3. Very fine.	1
475	1803 Another, from same dies as last. Good.	1
476	1836 Liberty setd, without stars. GOBRECHT on base ; fine, a few light scratches and trifling edge dents.	1
477	1859 O. mint. Extremely fine ; a few light nicks.	1
478	1896 Proof set. 5, 10, 25, 50c. and $1.	1
479	Gold Dollars. 1849 Unc., brilliant mint lustre.	1
480	1850 Very fine.	1
481	1851 Very fine.	1
482	1852 Extremely fine, sharp.	1
483	1853 Fine.	1
484	1854 Old type. Uncirculated, sharp, slight faint scratches on obv.	1
485	1855 Fine.	1
486	1855 O. mint. Fine.	1
487	1856 Italic 5. Extremely fine.	1
488	1857 Fine.	1
489	1861 Uncirculated.	1
490	1862 Uncirculated.	1
491	1870 Very fine.	1
492	1873 Fine.	1
493	1874 Unc. A faint scratch on obv.	1
494	1876 A proof, slightly impaired.	1
495	1878 Slightest marks of circulation ; brilliant.	1
496	1885 Faint scratch, otherwise unc.	1
497	1889 Fine.	1
498	Three Dollars. 1871 Fine.	1
499	1881 Fine.	1
500	1883 Very fine.	1
501	Gold Quarter Dol. 1855 Head *l.*, 10 stars. ℞ Value and date within wrth. Fine.	1

502   Gold Half Dols.   1864 Head *l.*, G. below, 13 stars. ℞ Value
      and date in wrth.   Octagonal.   Fine.   1
503   1871 Head *l.*, L. below, 13 stars and date.   ℞ Value in wrth.
      Proof.   1
504   Others.   1856 Half Dols.   Head *l.*, 13 stars.   ℞ Value and
      date in dotted circle.   Octagonal.   Fair and fine ; both holed.
      1870 Quarter Dol.   G. below head, 13 stars and date.   ℞
      Value in wrth.   Octag.   Fine ; piece broken from edge.
      1871 Half Dol., 10 stars.   ℞ Value and date in wrth ;
      holed, with ring.   Fine.   4
505   **Postal Currency.**   (New and crisp, unless otherwise stated.)
      1st issue, 5, 10, 25, 50c.   A. B. N. Co.   Perforated edges.   4
506   Another set as last, but with plain edges.   4
507   A strip of 4 unsevered 5c. notes, 1 creased to cut.   4
508   A strip of 3 unsevered 10c. notes.   3
509   25c.   Perforation slight at *r.* end, without A. B. N. Co.   1
510   50c.   Perforation wanting at *l.* end, without A. B. N. Co.   1
511   2d issue.   Washington in bronze oval. 5, 10, 25, 50c.   Bronze
      letters and figures on back.   4
512   50c. as last.   ℭ—1—18—63 on fibre paper.   1
513   3d issue.   3c., bust of Washington ; dark curtain.   1
514   3c. as last, with light curtain.   1
515   5c. Clark, 10c. Wash., 25c. Fessenden.   3
516   25c. Fessenden, with 25 in white on solid bronze.   Fibre paper.
      A few pin-point holes ; slight tear on right end ; nothing
      gone.   Possibly the rarest note in the series.   1
517   50c. Justice setd.   Plain paper, without bronze letters on back.   1
518   50c. Spinner.   Details as last.   1
519   50c. Spinner.   New design on back, 50 in centre.   1
520   *Red backs.*   5 Cents Clark.   1
521   10 Cents Washington.   1
522   25 Cents Fessenden.   1
523   50 Cents Justice setd, without gilt letters on back.   1
524   50 Cents Spinner.   1
525   *Red backs, autographic signatures.*   10c. Washington, signed by
      Colby & Spinner.   1
526   50c. Justice setd, without letters or figures on back, signed by
      Colby & Spinner.   1
527   50c. Spinner, signed by Colby & Spinner.   1

528 4th Issue. 15c. Columbia. Pink silk fibre paper.   1
529 25c. Washington. Pink silk fibre paper. 5th Issue. 10c.
    Meredith. Long and short key in Treasury seal.   3
530 25c. Walker, 50c. Crawford.   2
530a 15c. Grant and Sherman. Autographic signatures of Jeffries
    & Spinner. Separate front and green back, wide margins.
    Back torn ¼ inch, nothing gone, a few creases ironed out.   1
530b 15c. Grant and Sherman. As last, with red back, wide mar-
    gins, numerous creases well ironed out.   1
530c 15c. Grant and Sherman. Lithographic signatures, wide mar-
    gins, green back. A long tear from edge through ⅛ of the
    back, nothing gone, back also has creases ironed out.   1
531 *Colonial.* Maryland, 1770 $⅔, 1, 4, 6, 8; 1774 $⅓, ⅔, 4, 8.
    Good to fine, 5 are mended.   9
532 Old Bank Bills. North, South and West, $1, 3, 5, 10, 20, 50,
    100 (18). Northern Municipal War Issues. 5, 10 (2), 25c.
    (2). Mostly fine and choice.   23
533 Confederate States. Sept. 2d, 1861 to Feb'y 17th, 1864, 50c.
    to $500. Fine to new and crisp, most of last.   22
534 Alabama, 1863 25, 50c., $1, 1864 $100. Georgia, 1863-64 15c.
    to $100 (12). Louisiana, Missouri, No. Carolina, $1 to 20
    (9). Good to new and crisp.   25
535 Georgia. April 6th, 1864 $500. Fine.   1
536 Toronto. Agricultural Bank, Upper Canada. 20 Shillings
    Currency or Four Dollars, Oct. 1st, 1837. Fine.   1
537 **Foreign Silver.** Cuba. 1897 Souvenir Peso. Female hd *r.*
    PATRIA Y LIBERTAD ℞ REPUBLICA DE CUBA Arms. Unc.,
    sharp. 36.   1
538 Guadaloupe (1813). G crowned, on coins of Louis XV and
    XVI, size 18, 21, 26½, for 6, 12 and 24 Sous. Fine and very
    rare.   3
539 Guatemala. Chas. IV, 1789 Procl. Real. Horseman above
    2 mts. V. good, holed. 21.   1
540 Colombia. 1892 50 Ctvo, with bust of Columbus. V. gd. 30.   1
541 Pasco, Peru. 1844 4 Rls. Liberty stdg. ℞ Arms. Good. 34.   1
542 Sweden. Oscar II, 1897 2 Kronor commemorating the 25th
    year of his reign. Unc. 31.   1
543 Schaumburg-Lippe. Geo. William, 1857 Dble Thl. on the 25th
    year of his reign. V. fine and rare. Ger. Cats. list this pc.
    from 25 to 30 Marks. 41.   1

544   Indo-China. 1889 Sapèque and Cent in Æ, 10, 20, 50c. and
      1 Piastre. Æ. Unc., equal to proofs.   6

545   **Foreign Copper.** Canada. Magdalen Isl. 1815 Penny.
      Fine ; a few nicks.   1

546   1813 Trade & Navigation. Commerce setd. ℞ ONE | PENNY
      | TOKEN etc. V. fine ; medium olive.   1

547   1813 Field-Marshal Wellington. Mil. bust *l.*, date below. ℞
      ONE PENNY TOKEN Female setd *l.* on union jack, holds
      trident.   1

548   1813 Vimiera, Talavera, etc. Mil. bust *l.* ℞ Type as last,
      differently executed, with date in exergue. Nearly fine.   1

549   N.d. Bust sim. to last, with legend ending SALAMANCA ℞
      COSSACK — PENNY TOKEN A Cossack mtd *r.* V. fine.   1

550   N.d. Field-Marshal Wellington. Military bust *l.*, branches
      crossed below. ℞ ONE PENNY TOKEN. Female setd as in
      547, branches crossed below. V. fine ; dark olive.   1

551   1815 " Ships, Colonies and Commerce." ℞ FOR | PUBLICK |
      ACCOMMODATION Fine. Brass, 28.   1

552   Durango. 1851 ⅛ Real. Large 8°, one of the best I have
      seen. 18½.   1

553   Georgetown, Demarara. Middlemas Brothers & Co. Fine,
      rare. Brass. 24.   1

554   England. Geo. IV, 1826 Farthing. Unc., red. 1827 ⅛ Far.
      for Malta. Good. Wm. IV, 1835 ⅛ Far. as last. Fine.
      Vic., 1852 Far. Unc.   4

555   — Seventeenth Cent. Far. Tokens. Hy Noldred, GET IN YE
      ISLE OF TENNET. John Dyer of Minster, and a Sherborn
      Farthing for the Poor, 1669. Good.   3

556   Isle of Man. 1758 Athol, Duke, ½d. 1786 Geo. III, ½ and
      1d. The last fair, others fine.   3

557   1811 Bank Penny, poor; and Manx Penny, v. fair. 1813
      Geo. III, ½ and 1 Penny. 1830 " God save the King " ½d.
      1839 Vic., ½d. Fair to good.   6

558   France. 1st Rep., 5th year. Paris mint, 5 Centimes. Unc.,
      dark olive. 28.   1

559   Minorca. Alf. V, 1416–58 Head. ℞ Arms. Good. 15.   1

560   Gibraltar. 1802 2 Qts., 1810 1, 2 do., all Keelings ; 1820 2
      do., Spittles. Good to fine.   4

561   San Marino. 1875 10 Ctmi. Arms. V. good. 30.   1

562 Viterbo. 1796 2½ Bai. Bust of St. Peter. V. good. 30.   1

563 Greece. 1828 5, 10 Lepta ; 1830–31 1, 10 do. Gd to fine.   4

564 Tunis. 1281=1864–5 ¼ Caroub, one of the smallest of modern
    coins, and rare. Fine. 13½.   1

565 Zanzibar. (1881–90) Pesa. Scales. Fine. 25.   1

566 China. Ming Series, B. C. 317–228. Razor-shaped coin, 5½
    inches. Fine.   1

567 Manila. Ferd. VII, 1834 2 Quartos. Lion. R⁄ Arms. V.
    fair, rare. 26.   1

568 Russia. 1804 5 Kopecks, Ekaterinburg and Kolywan mints.
    Nearly fine. 44. 1805 1 Kopeck, K. mint. Good. 26.   3

569 **Medals.** Ferd. VII, 1808 Bust *l.* R⁄ " Pro solio," etc.
    Loop, oval floral attachment. Fine. Æ gilt, 37 x 45.   1

570 1809 Bust *l.* R⁄ Minerva seated before book-case. Perfect.
    Æ 49.   1

571 1809 Bust *r.* R⁄ General, Pope and Cardinal setd. Holed
    by loop. Good. Æ gilt, oval 37 x 45.   1

572 Maximilian, head *r.* by *A. Kleeburg.* R⁄ Angel beside tomb,
    1832–1867. Fon. 6705. V. fine, bril. W. m.   1

573 Guadalajara. Ferd. VII, 1809 Bust *r.* R⁄ Mars and Indian.
    V. fine, loop removed. Oval 37 x 41. Æ gilt.   1

Medals of the Freemasons.

I have for sale two copies of MARVIN'S "MASONIC MEDALS," fresh and handsomely bound in blue buckram, stamped in gold, and red edges. Long out of print.

Price, $12.00 per copy.

One copy, similarly bound, *very slightly* water-stained.

Price, $9.00.

It has been some years since this rare book could be obtained in fine condition. Only 160 copies were printed and twenty were destroyed in a fire. This is a rare opportunity.

LYMAN H. LOW.

330 PAGES, 18 PLATES, 1 IN COLORS.

VERBUM SAPIENTI SAT.

A Catalogue of this sale, with the prices realized, marked in red ink, will be mailed for 40c., prepaid.

A study of the prices at which coins and medals are selling cannot fail to make bidding more satisfactory. The cost is but a trifle, and a knowledge is thus rapidly acquired by comparison of the different sales, enabling the bidder to make offers which will enhance his chance of obtaining what is desired.

I can supply priced Catalogues of my sales for 1896–8, as follows : —

1896.

April 30. Mercantile Library, St. Louis. 454 lots. .35
June 23. Mason Fisher, of Fall River. 567 lots. .35
Oct. 15, 16. Nathan Belcher, of New London, Thos. H. Sheppard, of Pittsburgh, and others. 1252 lots. .75
Dec. 21. Johnston, Payne, Cunningham. 552 lots. .35

1897.

Feb. 4. A dealer discontinued, and a Pittsburgh collection. 594 lots. .35
April 12. Geo. F. Nesbitt, Brookeville, Md. 551 lots. .35
June 15. Henry C. Miller, New York, and others. 656 lots. .35
Aug. 10. A Physician's property, and others. 480 lots. .35
Oct. 23. Various Private Properties. 472 lots. .35

1898.

Jan. 11, 12. Benjamin Betts, of Brooklyn, N. Y. 1,183 lots, 5 plates. 1.00
May 23, 24. Col. Walter Cutting, of Pittsfield, Mass. 993 lots, 3 plates, $1.00.

Collectors will be materially aided in the pursuit and pleasures of Numismatics, and kept advised of the current events relating to the science, by subscribing to the "American Journal of Numismatics," published quarterly since 1866. Price, $2.00 per annum. Specimen numbers, 50 cents.

Subscriptions may be sent to W. T. R. Marvin, 73 Federal Street, Boston, or Lyman H. Low, 36 West 129th Street, New York.